THE WAY THROUGH THE GLENS

THE WAY THROUGH THE GLENS

Hamish MacInnes

Constable · London

First published in Great Britain 1989
by Constable and Company Limited
10 Orange Street London WC2H 7EG
Copyright © 1989 Hamish MacInnes
Set in Monophoto Photina 11pt by
BAS Printers Limited, Over Wallop, Hampshire
Printed and bound in Spain by
Graficas Estella S.A.

British Library CIP data
MacInnes, Hamish, *1930*–
The way through the glens
1. Scotland. Highlands. Description & travel
I. Title
914.11′504858

ISBN 0 09 469340 4

To the Scottish Highlands which have given me so much pleasure

INTRODUCTION

THIS circular, pictorial tour of the Highlands of Scotland takes you through some of its most stunning scenery, which can be reached by car or even bicycle from many comfortable hotels or Bed and Breakfast houses along the way. As the majority of visitors arrive through Glasgow or Edinburgh, I have made these two cities the start – or the finish, depending which way round you wish to proceed.

This book is not a step-by-step text for 'doing' the Highlands. It is more of a companion to take along as you travel, to steer you via scenic glens or castles steeped in history. I hope that when you return home it will serve as a reminder, a memento of your visit to Scotland.

It is only right that we should begin our tour from the capital, Edinburgh, the Athens of the North. Indeed it resembles Athens in many ways, having a similar geographical layout. Central Edinburgh was the site of an active volcano some 325 million years ago: this is where Arthur's Seat now stands. The resistant vent-plugs of agglomerate and lava stand as prominent natural landmarks.

The history of Edinburgh would fill several volumes, as would a description of its architecture, yet one doesn't feel lost here, for it is a compact and friendly city where most of the historical sites are within walking distance of the main thoroughfare, Princes Street. It is a place to linger, to spend at least a couple of days seeing the sights – and longer if you wish to take in the Festival activities in August.

As our tour is essentially of the country rather than of towns, let us first go west and north past Stirling, where the Wallace Monument stands as a lasting memorial to one of Scotland's most revered sons, William Wallace who led the successful rout of the English King Edward I's invading army in 1297. Stirling Castle, too, has a prominent place in Scottish history. Its role before the twelfth century is somewhat obscure, but it is known that King Alexander I died here in 1124.

We continue to Doune, and to Callander on the fringe of the Trossachs, both of which villages are worth lingering in. Doune was famous at one time for pistol- and sporran-making; it still boasts the two-arched bridge, founded in 1535 by Robert Spittal, tailor to Margaret, the Queen of James IV. There is also the eleventh-century Doune Castle, standing aloof and apparently eternal above the river Teith. Callander is a good centre for exploring the Trossachs, that miniature Scottish Lake District so beloved of Sir Walter Scott. It is a bustling village justly popular with weekending Glaswegians. At Callander there is also a camp of the Roman general Agricola (AD 80).

Heading north-westwards towards Crianlarich we join the A82 from Glasgow, Scotland's biggest city. Like Edinburgh, Glasgow is rich in history and its university was founded in 1450, making it the second oldest in Scotland. In recent times Glasgow has undergone a renaissance. The old image of the city has been demolished along with its slums and ghettos; the architecture of this ancient merchant port has had an exciting face-lift; the place is vibrant with renewed culture and commerce. In some ways it has outstripped its old rival, Edinburgh, in both.

From Glasgow you can go 'doon the Water' to the island of Arran. The ferry plies from Ardrossan to Brodick and from Claonaig to Lochranza. It is an island well worth visiting, with lovely walks and stunning scenery. Brodick is Arran's principal town.

Access to the north and west of Scotland is easy from Glasgow, via the A82. This highway snakes along the edge of Loch Lomond, one of Scotland's most beautiful and famous lochs: once a very tortuous road, it has now been improved and widened, but is still one of the most scenic routes in the country. This was the country of the outlaw Rob Roy MacGregor, who was a sort of eighteenth-century Rambo.

At Tarbet we must consider alternative routes to the Highlands, for here (the point at which the Viking raiders used to transport their longboats overland to Loch Long) the A83 branches westwards and will also take us north, though more circuitously. It goes first to Inveraray, the seat of the Clan Campbell, a once-hated and feared clan, and continues to Campbeltown which (though now not overrun with Campbells) perches on the tip of the Mull of Kintyre.

From Inveraray we make for Oban via one of two spectacular routes. The longer is by way of Lochgilphead on the A816: it has several fine stopping-off places, such as Crinan, with its canal that in summer sports a flotilla of yachts. Nearby, on the Great Moss, is the ancient capital of the region of Dalriada, the fort of Dunadd. Virtually all that is now left is the knoll on which the fort once stood, but this was the cradle of Scottish history.

A shorter route to Oban, whose name is Gaelic for 'the small creek', leaves Inveraray by the A819 to Dalmally, and then joins the Tyndrum road from the east, the A85, which

leads to Oban via the Pass of Brander, where both Robert the Bruce and William Wallace staged successful ambushes.

Oban, a mecca for tourists, is one of the finest harbours on the western seaboard, and though there are ample scenic delights within easy motoring or walking range, it is above all the sea that beckons. Ferries will take you to a myriad of islands – to Mull, Iona, Colonsay, Tiree, Coll, Lismore and the Outer Isles among them.

Oban was a settlement from early times, and remains of Azilian man (about 6000 BC) have been excavated from where George St now stands. Above the town is McCaig's Folly, a rotunda built to a design inspired by the Coliseum of Rome. It is a tribute to John Stuart McCaig, a local worthy, who constructed it to give work to the unemployed between 1890 and 1900.

Ancient Dunollie Castle, on the north arm of Oban Bay, was a stronghold of the MacDougalls, a family descended from the Norse-Celtic Dougall, King of the South Isles and eldest son of Somerled, King of the Isles, who died in 1164. The existing castle dates from before the fifteenth century, but long before that a fort existed here: there are records of the early fortifications being burned then rebuilt on three separate occasions between 685 and 700. Close by is the MacDougall mansion, and the original clan still owns the estate.

Mull is one of the finest islands off the west coast of Scotland. It seems to have infinite variety, with high hills, moorlands and woods, and it is big enough for you to stretch your legs and to forget that it is, in fact, an island. It is also eminently accessible: you can get there by a car ferry from Oban, or from Morvern where a smaller ferry, which also takes cars, plies between Lochaline in Morvern and Fishnish on Mull.

Tobermory, with 800 inhabitants, is the

principal town – in fact, the only town on Mull. The population of the entire island is only 3,000. Tobermory is a snug little place crowding round a natural harbour. In Tobermory Bay lies the wreck of a Spanish galleon, an armed merchant ship known as a carrack. She was the *Santa Maria della Grazia e San Giovanni Battista*, and was commandeered by the Spanish, complete with captain and crew, as part of the Spanish Armada. She put into Tobermory in 1588 after the dispersal of the Armada and was blown up in the bay, some say by a British agent. However, the exact truth is still a mystery. It was widely rumoured also that there was treasure aboard when she went down, and over the years there have been various unsuccessful attempts at salvaging her.

Many famous sons of Mull have made their mark in history. Gruline was the birthplace of Major-General Lachlan MacQuarrie, first Governor of New South Wales and known as the 'Father of Australia'.

On the west of Mull, separated from it only by a narrow channel, is the island of Iona. Its original name was the Norse 'I', which simply means 'island'. Iona today is still a place of pilgrimage, for Christianity originally was taken from here to mainland Scotland. St Columba was not the first Irish saint to set foot on Iona, but it was he who set up his headquarters on the island with his Brethren of Columba, after landing at Port na Curaich on the south coast of the island on 12 May 563. He brought with him from Ireland a vow: not to return to his homeland until he had gained as many souls for Christ as had perished in the Battle of Cooldrevny, for which he held himself responsible.

Just north of Oban, at Dunbeg, stands Dustaffnage Castle, whose name means 'the fort of the seaweed'. It has had an interesting past and nearby, on a grassy knoll by the head of the bay, was another ancient fort where the Stone of Destiny was kept before it was taken to Kenneth McAlpin's coronation in 844.

A short way to the south-west of the castle is a thirteenth-century chapel, where various Daldriadic kings were laid to rest beneath the floor. In 1463 a bizarre event occurred close to this holy place. Dugald was the bastard son of John Stewart, Lord of Lorne, the result of his Lordship's infatuation with a fifteen-year-old MacLaren girl. As he had no legitimate sons, he wished to set things right legally for young Dugald. But human nature was no different then from now, especially where the Campbells were involved. Three daughters of the Lord of Lorne had married Campbells, and the Campbells knew that they would lose any claim to the Lordship if his marriage to Dugald's mother took place. To avoid personal involvement, they hired a hit-man, one Alan MacCoull, an illegitimate and nefarious kinsman of the MacDougalls.

On the wedding day the Lord of Lorne emerged from Dunstaffnage with a handful of lightly armed companions and made his way to the chapel to join his bride. Alan MacCoull's gang ambushed them, many of the wedding group were slaughtered, and the Lord of Lorne, badly stabbed, was left for dead. Alan MacCoull and his heavily armed men now went for the castle and captured it. However, the Lord of Lorne was not yet dead, and at the insistence of the priest was hurriedly carried into the chapel and married to the MacLaren girl. He died an hour later. Despite this, however, Campbells eventually did take over most of Lorne.

Heading north towards Glen Coe the A828 passes over Connel Bridge, beneath which are the Falls of Lora, named after an early Celtic hero, Laoighre. They are tidal falls created by a submarine reef. At Appin is Castle Stalker, or Stalcair, which means 'hunter', standing with its feet in the water on the north side of Loch

Laich. It has stood thus since the thirteenth century, and was patronized by James IV during his tour of the Western Isles.

It was at Tarbet that I suggested alternative routes north and west and from there it is the A82 from Glasgow to Inverness which is the main road northwards. It passes through Crianlarich, and continues to Glencoe after negotiating the wilds of the Moor of Rannoch, a desolate yet beautiful peatland with lochs like dark mirrors. At one time this was the cradle of a vast glacier, and later it was clothed in forest, the forest of Caledon. Preserved tree roots can still be seen in the peat, which is up to 19 ft (6 m) deep in places. It is said that guides used to be available in olden times to lead travellers through the great forest, which covered some 56 square miles (80 square km) and extended as far as Braemar and Loch Affric. It probably still existed as recently as Roman times, and how it disappeared is a mystery. Some hold that the Viking policy of burning forests, no doubt to flush out dissenters, was the cause; another theory is that it was burned to rid the region of wolves. In any case, there is evidence of burning in the area from early times.

Glen Coe has a profound effect on some people, who find it claustrophobic and frightening, hemmed in, as it is, by the steep flanks of the mountains, as if demons were lying in ambush. Charles Dickens had misgivings of this kind when he scuttled through it in 1841. Others find the Glen a place of charm, changing from season to season, hour to hour. Even in torrential rain it is fascinating, with ribbons of waterfalls plunging headlong to the valley floor.

The name Coe, from which the river that runs through it also takes its name, is obscure, but the Glen was a place of turbulence long before the infamous Massacre of 1692 – of which more later. The Glen Coe Cauldron Subsidence was the original cause of this great upthrust of cliffs and peaks, and the region was subsequently eroded by ice in the form of huge glaciers which were mainly fed from what is now known as the Moor of Rannoch to the east. The Cauldron Subsidence, or ring fault, can be most easily understood by imagining a roughly circular fracture not dissimilar in effect to a loose cork in the neck of a bottle. With the descent of the 'cork', magma from the earth's core was squeezed up through the gap and cooled to form an annular (ring-shaped) sheet of granite. The ring fault can still be seen as the Chasm of An t'Sron, just to the south-west of Loch Achtriochtan, and continuing as Clachaig Gully above the Clachaig Inn. The River Etive forms the other edge of the ring fault.

One of the great architects of the Scottish Highlands was the Ice Age which lasted in Scotland for some 10,000 years. In Glen Coe the ice sheets stood higher than today's mountain tops. Blocks of granite which can be seen at nearly 3,000 ft (900 m) on the Aonach Eagach Ridge were carried there by the ice from the great ice basin at the Moor of Rannoch. The side valleys, too, had their own supply of ice, forming smaller glaciers and swelling the mainstream. It would be difficult to find a more perfectly glaciated valley than the Lairig Gartain, between Buachaille Etive Beag and Buachaille Etive Mor at the eastern end of Glen Coe.

At the eastern approaches to the Glen stands Kingshouse Hotel. As well as being a notorious haunt of smugglers it used to be a 'stance' in the days when black cattle were driven (hence 'droving') from the north and west of Scotland to markets, or trysts as they were called, in Crieff and Falkirk. ('Ba' is the Gaelic word for cattle, and Ba Cottage is the next stance on the route to Crieff, on the southern edge of the Moor of Rannoch.) Kingshouse Hotel is one of the oldest licensed establishments in Scotland, and it commands a wonderful position with stunning views of Buachaille Etive Mor.

Today the hotel is equipped with all comforts usually demanded by a sybaritic society; but this was not so in Dorothy Wordsworth's time (the early nineteenth century). She thought it looked quite inviting from a distance: '. . . but when we came close to it the outside forewarned us of the poverty within. Scarce a blade of grass could be seen growing upon the open ground . . . Never did I see such a miserable, such a wretched place, long rooms with ranges of beds, no other furniture except benches, or perhaps one or two crazy chairs . . . the floors were far dirtier than an ordinary house could ever be if they were never washed.' Dorothy's complaints did not end there: '. . . dinner was a shoulder of mutton so hard that it was impossible to chew the little flesh that might be scraped off the bones, and some sorry soup made of barley and water, for it has no other taste. After supper the woman, after having first asked us if we slept in blankets, brought in two pairs of sheets, which she begged that I would air by the fire, for they should be dirtied downstairs. I was very willing, but behold the sheets were so wet, that it would have been at least a two-hours' job before a far better fire than could be mustered at Kingshouse.'

A branch road goes southwards to Glen Etive from the A82 close to Kingshouse. This is a tranquil glen and well worth a visit, though there is no through route to Connel at the mouth of Loch Etive. It was here in ancient times that Deirdre of the Sorrows lived with her lover Naisi, after fleeing Ulster and King Connor's anger. They were later lured back to Ireland to their premature deaths. A sad ballad, 'Deirdre's Farewell', composed by Deirdre on their fateful return voyage, depicts the subtle beauty of this wonderful glen at dawn.

As you descend into Glen Coe the left-hand side of the valley is dominated by three peaks, now popularly known as the Three Sisters: Beinn Fhada, Gearr Aonach and Aonach Dubh. The Lost Valley (Coire Gabhail in Gaelic) occupies the gap between the first two lovely ladies. This is the Coire of the Plunder and it was here that the MacDonalds of Glen Coe hid their stolen cattle. Cattle-reiving was a national sport in olden times – indeed, reiving was to prove the downfall of the Glen Coe MacDonalds.

The Massacre of Glen Coe took place 'at five o'clock precisely' on the morning of 13 February 1692. The crime was a particularly heinous one, the murder of their hosts by Redcoats who until that moment had been guests. 'Murder under trust' was an abominable crime under old Scots law.

The Massacre had its roots in the MacDonalds' chequered history. A contemporary record describes the clan as practising 'open and manifest oppression, murder, sorning and theft'. Sorning was obtaining dinner, bed and breakfast by force or threats. In those days such pastimes were practised by most Highland clans, but unfortunately for the MacDonalds they happened to be geographically close to the powerful Clan Campbell, and it was the Campbells who were the prime movers in the atrocity of 1692.

About thirty-eight men, women and children lost their lives on that cold morning and many others died while escaping through the adjoining glens in the teeth of a severe blizzard. MacIain, the ageing Chief, was murdered together with his wife, and the clan never really recovered from this blow. A memorial to MacIain stands close to the village of Glencoe, and the Chief and other members of the MacDonald clan are buried on Eilean Munde, the burial isle on Loch Leven.

Beyond Ballachulish Bridge (a sad structure in steel, quite out of keeping with the surroundings), we continue for a short way as far as Corran Ferry. Ardgour and the regions on the other side of the Corran Narrows of Loch Linnhe are gems well worth visiting, but it is surprising how a narrow strip of water can deter a tourist invasion, for only a small percentage of travellers venture into this 'empty quarter'. The area has everything the lover of outdoors can desire: mountains, lochs, sea, moors and castles. Garbh Bheinn, the principal mountain of Ardgour, is composed of gabbro which rivals that of the Cuillin of Skye.

It is from Lochaline in Morvern that the alternative ferry to Mull runs, and at the tip of this ragged part of the western seaboard is isolated Ardnamurchan Point, the most westerly point of the British mainland. The road that leads to it is narrow and tortuous, and those used to six-lane freeways may have cardiac arrest at the mere prospect. However, standing at Ardnamurchan lighthouse on a stormy day gives one a feeling of being on the edge of the earth. It is 23 miles (41 km) west of Land's End, and its name means 'point of the great ocean' (or possibly point of the sea-hounds – probably a reference to otters). Nearby are sandy Sanna and the Great Eucrite, this latter being a most impressive ring dyke, 1 mile (1.6 km) in annular width. However, it is difficult to identify unless you ascend Meall Sanna or one of the other surrounding hills. Ardnamurchan peninsula was a stepping-stone by which Christianity came to the mainland, and it is here that St Ciarnan was laid to rest in 548.

If you continue on the A861 from Corran Ferry rather than deviating west to Ardnamurchan, you reach the village of Acharacle. The 'Ach' is pronounced as if you are clearing your throat. Here the tail-end of Loch Shiel narrows into the River Shiel, and spills into the Atlantic close to Tioram Castle, a dignified pile which can be well viewed from a lovely beach at the end of the road which follows the river's east bank.

Beyond, at the head of Loch Moidart, which boasts of a superb view of the Island of Eigg, are the Seven Men of Moidart. These are trees which stand as a memorial to the fleet-footed Prince Charles Edward Stuart's seven companions who landed with him at nearby Loch nan Uamh on 25 July 1745. By taking an old funeral road over the hill to Loch Shiel (you can also drive round it) you arrive at Dalelia. Here it is sometimes possible to hire a boat, and if you can it is well worth visiting the island of Eilean Fhionnan, named after St Finnan. The remains of his cell can still be seen on the island, as can his unique square-mouthed bronze bell. The island occupies a magnificent setting and it would be difficult to imagine a more fitting place for worship and contemplation.

However, as we are close to the A830, the Fort William–Mallaig road, at this point, let us next visit Fort William.

Like Glen Coe, the Fort William district of Lochaber has a history of battles and bloodshed. Fort William is no longer a 'Wild West' town but a hub of tourism, in which it ranks equal with Oban in importance, though not as a port. It stands at a natural crossroads where the road north is intersected to that leading west, via Loch Eil and Glen Finnan, to the port of Mallaig at the western edge of Inverness. Glen Finnan is where the standard was raised at the start of the 1745 Rebellion against the British Crown, which was to end in ignominious defeat at Culloden for Prince Charlie and the Jacobite cause. You can also reach Mallaig by rail, an extremely scenic route on which British Rail now operates a steam train during the summer months.

Ferry boats from Mallaig harbour go 'over the sea to Skye', though the more popular route for vehicles these days is from Kyle of Lochalsh to the north. From the quaint fishing port of Mallaig and also its close neighbour, Arisaig, boats leave for the islands of Muck,

Rhum, Canna and Eigg. If you have time to spare, these island hops are well worth doing, for they are day voyages which will linger in your memory. There is also a small ferry boat from Mallaig to Knoydart, a remote and beautiful 'no man's land' of rock and mountain sandwiched between Loch Nevis and Loch Hourn.

Fort William takes its name from the fort which used to stand there, but the modern town hasn't won any laurels for fine architecture or tasteful planning. It is somewhat nondescript compared with Oban, yet it is an excellent centre for holiday operations, and what it lacks in aesthetic appeal is more than made up for by the surrounding country. Glen Nevis and the banks of the River Lochy both are excellent places to stroll – by the latter, 3 miles (4.8 km) up on the right bank, are the ruins of Torcastle, once the seat of Banquo, Thane of Lochaber, immortalized in Shakespeare's *Macbeth*. Banquo's Walk follows the wooded river above idyllic pools.

The name Fort William is almost synonymous with that of Ben Nevis, which rises a short way to the south-east of the town, though it cannot be seen from there. It is a somewhat ungainly mass, akin to the proverbial fat lady. But it is a formidable mountain despite its relatively low altitude of 4,408 ft (1,344 m) and subject to such violent storms that the tourist path to the summit can be treacherous even in summer, if engulfed in a snowstorm or dense mist. It is the highest mountain in Britain and a popular venue of mountaineers who climb on its north-east face. It was here, and in nearby Glen Coe, that modern technical ice-climbing developed. An observatory was established on the summit of the 'Ben', as it is known locally, and was operative for twenty years, being abandoned in 1904. Later an hotel was opened, but that too has long since closed. The highest rainfall recorded at the observatory was in 1898 when 240 inches (60960 mm) fell! The name 'Nevis' is somewhat obscure, but it possibly means 'venomous one', which would seem an appropriate title since climbers and walkers perish on it each year. Incidentally, the West Highland Museum in Fort William is worth a visit, as is Inverlochy Castle near whose ruins is the site of the Earl of Montrose's famous victory over the Campbells in 1644.

To the north-east of Fort William runs the Great Glen, and a great glen it surely is with its Caledonian Canal joining hands with a string of lochs and rivers to make an impressive waterway connecting the Atlantic with the North Sea, and Fort William with Inverness. It was started by that innovative engineer Thomas Telford in 1803, and took nineteen years to complete.

The Great Glen Fault is an unique geological feature, the area to the north of the Glen being displaced 65 miles (104 km) to the south-west, relative to the land to the south. Weak tremors are occasionally felt there today.

We continue on our journey, still using the A82 after our possible deviations, and follow the Great Glen as far as Invergarry. Here we have two alternatives. First, we can head westwards on the A87 to the Isle of Skye, or branch off it at Loch Alsh to gain the wild country of Applecross and Torridon to the north. Or we can continue up the side of the Canal and its famous lochs – Loch Lochy, and Loch Ness – to reach Inverness. Let us take the former route: after 'doing' Skye, we can complete a quick circuit of the Northern Highlands to reach Inverness from the north-west.

The most significant attraction after passing through Glen Shiel, with its Five Sisters forming the northern wall of the glen, is Eilean Donan Castle. If you take the alternative car-ferry to Skye by crossing the Mam Ratagan pass to Kylerhea, you will miss this impressive fortress, though you could take it in on the way back by returning from Skye via the Kyle of Lochalsh–Kyleakin ferry.

The castle is in a splendid location at the meeting of three lochs, Loch Long, Loch Duich and Loch Alsh. It is seen at its best in the late evening during a good sunset, when its walls turn to a deep crimson. On more than one occasion blood also ran down those curtain walls. Loch Duich is named after an eleventh-century saint, St Dubhthach, but the castle itself was built on St Donan's Isle. This gentleman, too, was a religious and met an untimely death when he was murdered on the Island of Eigg in 616.

A vitrified fort stood on Eilean Donan before the original castle was built there 700 years ago. In 1719 during the ill-fated Jacobite rising the castle was destroyed, and it was rebuilt to its present glory in 1932 after a twenty-year restoration programme costing £250,000. The castle is open to the public. Like Glen Coe, Iona and Torridon, Kintail is owned by the National Trust for Scotland, an organization that preserves these superb regions for the nation.

The misty Isle of Skye casts a spell over many people. It has a strange quality, a softness and an air of mystery, about it. The Vikings called it Skuyo, 'cloud island', but it is known to the Gaels as Ant-Eilean Sgiathanach, 'the winged isle'. A glance at the map will show you how it got this name, with its many peninsulas and headlands. But with the Norsemen occupying Skye and the north and west coast of Scotland for three centuries, they inevitably left behind them a legacy of their place-names.

Portree is the main town on Skye. It means 'king's fort', and was given this title after a visit by James V in 1540. It was here, too, at what is now the Royal Hotel, that Prince Charlie said his last farewell to that Highland heroine, Flora MacDonald.

The Cuillin of Skye are splendid mountains, and are colour coded Black and Red. The latter are reddish hills to the east, divided by Glen Sligachan from the Black Cuillin. The latter are spectacular by any standards, and curl tightly, in an enormous horseshoe of gabbro, round Loch Coruisk, a loch which is hidden from view unless you scale the heights or reach it over a narrow isthmus from Loch Scavaig (take a boat from Elgol, and it is only a short walk from the edge of Loch Scavaig). Loch Coir'Uisg means 'corrie of the water', a name which is certainly applicable in the frequent torrential rain. The highest peak on Skye is Sgurr Alasdair at 3,257 ft (993 m), named after Sheriff Nicholson of Portree who made the first ascent.

Dunvegan Castle is a must for anyone interested in the history of the island. (It is interesting even to those who are not interested in history!) There were previously two main clans on Skye, the MacDonalds and the MacLeods. Dunvegan is the seat of the Clan MacLeod, and it has been so continuously for 700 years. Before that it was the site of a Norse fortress. It has all the historical props one could desire, from a damp and chilly dungeon to the legendary Fairy Flag – the Bratach Sith, a device of great power, capable of bringing herring into the loch, ensuring victory in battle and (if spread on the Chief's bed) of guaranteeing an heir. The Fairy Flag is believed to have been a consecrated banner of the Knights Templar, captured from the Saracens during the Crusades.

The top 'wing' of Skye is called Trotternish, and is a weird geological area where one can easily imagine goblins gambolling. It is called the Quiraing, a Gaelic name which means the 'pillared cattle-pen'. It is worth hiking into this strange place, for it takes only half an hour or so from below the zigzags on the Stafflin–Uig road. Further down the coast from Staffin is Storr, with its upright Old Man of Storr, a conspicuous landmark.

As I suggested back at Invergarry (page 13), it is possible to continue further north on the mainland from near Kyle of Lochalsh. The A890 snakes over the hill to descend to Loch Carron, or you can take an even more view-filled route via Plockton. At one time a ferry operated across Loch Carron, but now the road clings to the lochside with the scenic railway line to Kyle of Lochalsh sandwiched between. To gain the village of Loch Carron on the opposite shore, you turn left at the T-junction near the head of the loch. The A896 continues, one feels reluctantly, towards Achnasheen, a village which lives up to its name, 'field of rain'. Continuing on this route takes you south once more via Inverness.

Going north from Loch Carron the 'main road' (the A896) crosses a pass to Kishorn, where, at the head of Loch Kishorn, an even narrower road toils in a wide slalom over Bealach na Ba, the 'pass of the cattle', to drop to the west coast of Applecross. Though this is not the most direct route to Torridon, it is a deviation par excellence and you can join up with the A896 once more just short of Shieldaig village. This region is, in my opinion, one of the most striking in Britain. It presents a blend of loch, heather and rock in subtle tones, and imparts a tranquillity akin to that of a great cathedral with no walls.

Glen Torridon is a one-sided glen, with the majestic hulk of Liathach rearing to the north. It demands neck-craning effort to view its giddy sandstone terraces and castellated ridge. With four of its summits wearing quartzite caps, it is well named 'the grey one'. A reptilian road doubles back along Loch Torridon's north shore, stealing through the quaint village of Fasag to reach the road's end beyond the Pass of the Wind at Diabaig. Here, once upon a time, Viking longboats anchored. Diabaig is a mere cluster of houses crowding a small jetty; it is set on the edge of a bowl of gneiss which forms a natural harbour, and the surrounding rose-coloured rock is some of the oldest in the world.

The next stage of the Odyssey northwards on the A896 takes us beyond Liathach and its sister with seven heads, Beinn Eighe, which means 'file'. We now reach the one-horse village of Kinlochewe nestling at the south-east end of Loch Maree. Here too, at the T-junction, is an opportunity to deviate from our northerly progression by taking the A832 eastwards to Garve and Inverness. But if you have time, I recommend carrying on along the side of Loch Maree to Gairloch and Poolewe, for this is scenery which deserves an Oscar. Everything now seems more spacious, partly because of the magnificent road sweeping through the Caledonian pines that adorn the south side of the loch. On the far shore is some of the remotest country in Europe, with the mass of Slioch, 'the spear', 3,217 ft (980 m) high, rising like an extinct volcano above Loch Maree.

For those with an interest in greenery and blossom, Inverewe Gardens is a must. It is run by the National Trust for Scotland and is a permanent tribute to Osgood MacKenzie who, starting in 1862, created this oasis out of a windswept wilderness of rock and peat, on which only one three-foot-high willow bush grew. It is now one of the most famous gardens in the land.

After Inverewe the road takes you along the edge of Loch Ewe to Gruinard Bay. With its palm trees – such as also flourish at Inverewe – Gruinard could vie with any tropical paradise – if only the temperature were a few degrees warmer. It is a coast of sand and rock; inland the ground climbs to An Teallach, 'the forge', whose highest summit is Bidean a Ghlas Thuill at 3,484 ft (1,062 m). An Teallach is one of the most spectacular peaks in Scotland.

Beyond Dundonnell Hotel on Little Loch Broom the road climbs to more than 1000 ft

(304 m) and affords glimpses of An Teallach from what used to be Destitution Road, built in 1851 during the potato famine.

We join the A835 at Braemore Junction, which offers nothing but the road junction itself. A short way towards Ullapool, however, is the Corrieshalloch Gorge, sculpted by meltwater from the great ice cap, several thousand feet thick, which long ago lay to the south. There is a car-park on the other side of the road, and it is well worth the few minutes it takes to view the spectacular gorge.

We will make Ullapool on the shores of Loch Broom our final stop on this journey, otherwise we will find ourselves running out of both time and road. It is possible, in any case, to explore the northernmost reaches of Scotland by car from this busy port in a day. The town of Ullapool (its Norse meaning is 'Ulli's steading') is built on a late Ice Age beach 50 ft (15 m) above sea level. The town is relatively new, having been founded by the British Fisheries Society in 1788. Today fish still play an important role in its economy: indeed, in the autumn Loch Broom appears congested with Eastern European factory ships which descend on it each year. Some of the local shopkeepers have acquired a smattering of Russian from their frequent trading with the crews. Like Oban and Uig on Skye, it is also a port for ferries to the Outer Isles.

The highway north, the A835, is a good one, giving the driver time to absorb the scenery. Here there is elbow room between the mountains, and a feeling of infinite space. Various safaris are available, all of top quality. For example, beyond the imposing Ben More Coigach just north of Ullapool, a side road scuttling under the ramparts of Stac Polly continues to Achiltibuie. This is a lazy little village clinging to the bay like high-rise flotsam, with breathtaking views to the Summer Isles. There is much to see all over this part of Scotland, and you will find your

time here flying. (It is said in this locality that the word 'mañana' conveys a sense of urgency!) An equally narrow road goes up to Lochinver from the Achiltibuie highway. This offers views of the great peaks of Cul More and Cul Beag to the east, and vistas northwards to Suilven, at 2,399 ft (731 m) probably Scotland's most imposing mountain when viewed across the bay from Lochinver.

Lochinver is in Sutherland, which meant the 'south land' to the Vikings. It is a busy little port and one popular with discriminating anglers, having excellent lochs and rivers. Though I suggested the Achiltibuie–Lochinver deviation, you can in fact continue from Ullapool to Lochinver directly by turning left at Ledmore Junction and taking the A837. This road gives superb views of Suilven from Elphin and across Loch Assynt. At Loch Assynt the main road north, which becomes the A894, goes directly across the hill to Kylestrome Bridge.

From close to Lochinver an alternative, car-width, road takes you on a roller-coaster of bends and bays up the coast past Stoer and Nedd to join with the A894 close to Unapool. Here, until recent times, a ferry plied, but the elegant Kylestrome Bridge replaces it. There's not a great deal further north that you can go from here without getting wet, but a visit to Handa Island is worth considering. This is a bird sanctuary and an exciting place to explore, especially during the nesting period in spring. You can reach it from either Scourie or Tarbet.

Further on, there is another road junction at Rhiconich: the main road, such as it is, continues north and east of our remit to Durness, but the B801 leads off at this fork to Kinlochbervie, a thriving white-fish port. Nearby are the crofting communities of Oldshore More and Oldshore Beg, places out of another age. From here, too, if you feel energetic, a track leads north-east a little way past Oldshore Mor, and in 4 miles (6.4 km) reaches Sandwood Bay. This beach, big enough for a 747 to land on, is guarded at the southerly end by Am Buachaille, a rock stack. Sandwood is bordered by white bands of surf, and to the north and west there is nothing but ocean and more ocean. It is an awe-inspiring and beautiful place.

We must now return south, initially the way we have come, on reasonably good roads, which lead us to Inverness. Inverness is the capital of the north, a pleasant town lazily divided by the River Ness, which flows from the loch of that name, the last major loch in the chain of the Caledonian Canal before the North Sea.

If you have to hot-foot it home, the A9 offers a rapid route south, over the Pass of Drumochter. Much of General Wade's original old military road over the Pass is still visible. Further south, Blair Atholl is just off the A9: the village itself, and more especially Blair Castle, are worth a visit. However, allow time to savour the Castle's splendours, for a cursory visit will mean you will always hanker to see the rest. Anybody who was anybody in ancient times stayed here, and the oldest part of the castle is the Cumming's Tower which was probably built by Red Comyn about 1280. It was here that Viscount Dundee had his council of war before the Battle of Killiecrankie, a battle in which he was to lose his life.

The next pass south on the A9 is Killiecrankie, scene of that famous battle in 1689, when the Scots were victorious over William III's forces. The King's army was commanded by Major-General Hugh MacKay of Scourie who had 2,000 men killed and 500 taken prisoner. James Graham of Claverhouse, 'Bonnie Dundee', who led the Scots, died on the field. Near this pass the last wolf in Perthshire was killed in 1680.

Those not wishing to scuttle homewards via the A9 to Glasgow or Edinburgh will find the eastern Cairngorms and Deeside well worth exploring. This is country more placid than the Western Highlands: slopes angle gently down from rolling tops to the valleys, and the riverbanks, especially those away from the mountains, are often wooded. It is a region which has been, with good reason, patronized by royalty for generations. It is also a country of strongholds, which reflect more turbulent times. One should linger over this part of Scotland like a good glass of port, to savour its special qualities.

A network of roads intersects this area to the east of the Cairngorms and it is difficult to recommend any in particular, for they are all delightful. However, from the north a route via Granton-on-Spey to Tomintoul (perhaps taking in the Glenlivet distillery or one of the others on the 'Whisky Trail'), then going over the famous Lecht Road, makes a fitting approach to Royal Deeside.

After 'doing' the castles and perhaps some of the invigorating walks, you can leave this region from Braemar by taking the A93 over the Cairnwell, beside the ski complex. It now bypasses the Devil's Elbow, a notorious bend in earlier times. This road leads you down from the heathery wastes of Cairnwell into another world of trees and greenery at Blairgowrie.

I can suggest another diversion – to Glamis Castle. Take the Blairgowrie-Meigle road to this famous fifteenth-century castle, seat of the celebrated Lyon family for generations. Like Blair Castle, it is a place not to hurry over, and time is needed to browse through this treasure-house of history.

Undoubtedly some time-pressed visitors will by now have returned south, but may I suggest one further little tour that will take you to a part of Scotland quite different from what you have so far sampled? Take the A928 and A929 to Dundee (where Scott's ship *Discovery* now lies) and cross the Tay Road

Bridge to reach St Andrews, the seat of Scottish learning. The University was founded in 1403 and the construction of the Cathedral began in 1160. The Castle, said to have been erected 1188–1202, is also quite a place!

You can now continue to Edinburgh via the Forth Road Bridge by following the coastline of the East Neuk of the Kingdom of Fife. Here the fishing villages of Crail, Anstruther, Pittenweem and Elie offer you an aroma of fish and fairy-tale harbours, speaking volumes of the wind, storms and danger experienced by those to whom the North Sea is a way of life.

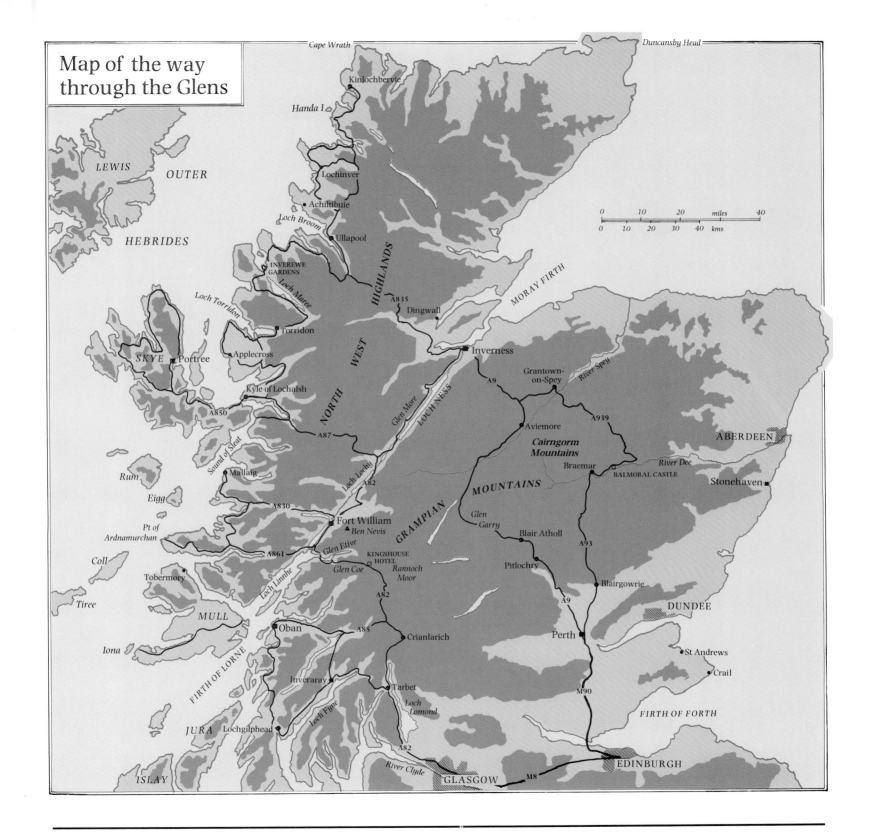

Map of the way through the Glens

Cape Wrath

Duncansby Head

Kinlochbervie

Handa I

LEWIS

OUTER

Lochinver

Achiltibuie

Loch Broom

Ullapool

HEBRIDES

INVEREWE GARDENS

Loch Maree

NORTH

WEST

HIGHLANDS

A835

Dingwall

MORAY FIRTH

Loch Torridon

Torridon

Inverness

Grantown-on-Spey

River Spey

SKYE

Portree

Applecross

A9

Kyle of Lochalsh

Glen More

LOCH NESS

Aviemore

A939

ABERDEEN

A850

A87

Cairngorm Mountains

Sound of Sleat

Loch Lochy

Braemar

River Dee

BALMORAL CASTLE

Rum

Mallaig

A82

MOUNTAINS

Stonehaven

Eigg

A830

Glen Garry

Pt of Ardnamurchan

Fort William

Ben Nevis

GRAMPIAN

Blair Atholl

A93

Coll

Glen Etive

KINGSHOUSE HOTEL

A861

Pitlochry

Tobermory

Glen Coe

Rannoch Moor

Loch Linnhe

A82

A9

Blairgowrie

Tiree

DUNDEE

MULL

Oban

A85

Crianlarich

Perth

St Andrews

Iona

FIRTH OF LORNE

Inveraray

Tarbet

Crail

Loch Lomond

M90

JURA

Loch Fyne

FIRTH OF FORTH

Lochgilphead

A82

ISLAY

River Clyde

EDINBURGH

GLASGOW

M8

miles

0   10   20   40

0   10 20 30 40   kms

[1] Edinburgh Castle

[2] The National Monument, Carlton Hill,
Edinburgh

[3] The Forth Rail Bridge

[4] Castle Doune

[5] Falls of Dochart

[6] Ben More above Crianlarich from Strath Fillan

[7] The Burrell Collection, Glasgow – a must for the visitor to Scotland

[8] University of Glasgow, the second oldest
university in Scotland

[9] Linlithgow Palace

[10] Goatfell, Arran, across Brodick Bay. The
Island of Arran can be reached by ferry from
Ardrossan.

[11] Loch Lomond

[12] Glen Orchy

[13] Inveraray Castle, seat of the Clan Campbell

[14] A 'heavy' contestant at Inveraray
Highland Games

[15] Crinan Canal

[16] Kilchurn Castle, Loch Awe

[17] Dunollie Castle, Oban

[18] Oban Harbour with McCaig's Folly above

[19] The village of Dervaig, Mull

[20] A Mull post box

[21] Iona, the cradle of Christianity, with the abbey

[22] The Kildalton High Cross, Islay

[23] Dunstaffnage Castle, near Oban

[24] Castle Stalker, Appin

[25] Looking towards Glen Coe from the Beinn a'Bheithir Ridge

[26] It was possibly here at his summer sheiling in Gleann Leac na Muidh that MacIain, the Chief of the MacDonalds of Glen Coe, was murdered in the Glen Coe Massacre of 1698.

THE MASSACRE OF GLENCOE
WITHIN THESE WALLS
MACIAIN CHIEF OF THE MACDONALDS, GLENCOE
WAS MURDERED ON THE MORNING
OF THE 13th FEBRUARY 1692.

[27] The memorial to MacIain, Chief of the Glen Coe MacDonalds, at Upper Carnach, Glen Coe

[28] The old road through Glen Coe, with the Three Sisters. the three stately peaks on the south side of the Glen

[29] The Aonach Eagach ridge and the River
Coe, Glen Coe

[30] Loch Leven and the Pap of Glen Coe

[31] Highland cattle

[32] The burial isle of the MacDonalds, Eilean
Munde, with Garbh Bheinn beyond

[33] The Peaks on the south side of Glen Coe,
Gearr Aonach and Aonach Dubh with Stob
Coire nan Lochan above the figure

[34] A pool in the River Coe, with Aonach Dubh behind

[35] The Mamores in spring snow, from Loch Leven

[36] Gearr Aonach, Glen Coe

[37] The paddle-steamer *Waverley* on Loch Linnhe

[38] The two Buachailles and the Lairig
Gartain from Glen Etive

[39] Corran Ferry with Ardgour on the other side

[40] Ardnamurchan Point, the most westerly
point of the British mainland

[41] The unique Celtic bronze bell at the ruins
of the church on Eilean Fhionnan, Loch Shiel

[42] The burial ground of the Macleans of
Ardgour, with Ben Nevis beyond

[43] The 'Iron Lady', the Fort William–Mallaig
steam train

[44] Mallaig harbour

[45] A lonely church on the road to Mallaig,
with Rois Bheinn behind

[46] The summit of Ben Nevis

[47] Ben Nevis from Corpach

[48] The parallel roads, Glen Roy

[49] Looking towards the peaks of Knoydart
from the Invergarry – Clunie road

[50] The Five Sisters of Kintail

[51] Eilean Donan Castle, Loch Duich

[52] Skye from Kylerhea

[53] The Cuillin from Elgol, Isle of Skye

[54] Isleornsay, Skye

[55] A Golden Eagle

[56] The Isles of Soay (foreground), Rhum and Canna from the Cuillin

[57] Neist Point with Neist Lighthouse. This is
the most westerly point on Skye

[58] The Inaccessible Pinnacle, Sgurr Dearg,
Cuillin

[59] Dunvegan Castle, seat of the Skye
MacLeods

[60] Duntulm Castle, Skye. The castle is
reputed to be haunted by a drunken ghost

[61] Sheep-shearing by hand, Skye

[62] En route to the Quiraing, North Skye

x

[63] The Quiraing and the 'Table'

[64] Kilt Rock, near Staffin, North Skye

[65] One of the 'men' of Storr, Skye

[66] Portree harbour, Isle of Skye

[67] The Cioch, Beinn Bhan, Applecross

[68] The only remaining 'Black House',
Applecross

[69] The perfect harbour of Diabaig, Loch Torridon

[70] Loch Torridon with Beinn Alligin

[71] A Fearnmore lamb, Applecross

[72] Slioch and Loch Maree

[73] Inverewe Gardens, Wester Ross

[74] The Peaks of Carnmore from Poolewe

[75] A view to the south-east from the
Poolewe–Dundonnell road

[76] The street clock, Ullapool

[77] Stac Polly

[78] The graveyard at Elphin

[79] Suilven and Lochinver

[80] A carpet of flowers, Handa Island

[81] Sandwood Bay

[82] Loch an Eilean, near Aviemore

[83] The Lairig Ghru, Cairngorms

[84] Corgarff Castle, Cock Bridge

[85] Making whisky, Glenlivet

[86] Shop closed, Strathdon

[87] Dark Lochnagar. This corrie is part of the Queen's Balmoral Estate. It has been a popular venue for royalty for decades, and was specially loved by Queen Victoria.

[88] Red deer in velvet

[89] On Royal Deeside

[90] No trekking today

[91] Stonehaven harbour

[92] Dunnottar Castle near Stonehaven

[93] St Andrews

[94] The breakwater at St Andrews, with the
Castle on the right

[95] Glamis Castle

[96] Crail Harbour

[97] The beech hedge on the A93, south of
Blairgowrie. This is Scotland's highest hedge.

[98] At Scone Palace